A Women's Study Guide of the Fruits of the

The
Abundant
Life

Susannah Rose Dorfsmith

ISBN: 978-1-933753-73-7

All Scripture quotations taken from the King James Version of the Bible

Susannah Rose Dorfsmith
Text and Cover design by Larisa Yoder

Carlisle Press
WALNUT CREEK

2673 Township Road 421
Sugarcreek, Ohio 44681
phone | 800.852.4482

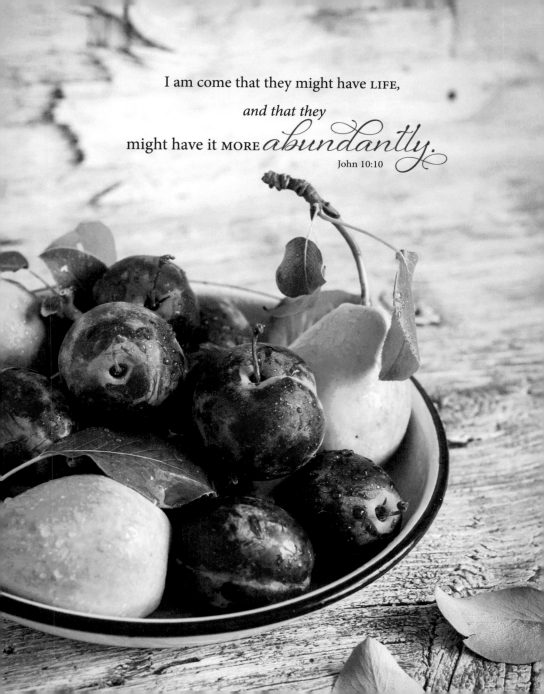

I am come that they might have LIFE,

and that they

might have it MORE *abundantly.*

John 10:10

Dedication

To those who yearn after the abundant life. May the fruit of God's Spirit flourish in you!

Introduction

Dear Readers,

Doesn't the word *abundant* sound appealing? I picture an established orchard, its sturdy trees faithfully bearing fruit for its owner. Such a scene speaks of purpose and fulfillment.

Deep inside, I find a longing to be abundant too. What would life be like if I could be, though on an exceedingly more important level, as flourishing as an established orchard? Is such a thing possible?

Yes! In John 10:10, Jesus says: *I am come that they might have life, and that they might have it more abundantly.* God wants to bring me from barren to bountiful, pointless to purposeful.

Does your heart cry out with mine for such a life? Then please join me in searching the Scriptures. Together, may we gain a deeper understanding of the abundance God holds out to each of us.

In His service,

Susannah Rose Dorfsmith

For the fruit of the *Spirit* is in all *goodness* and *righteousness* and *truth*.

Ephesians 5:9

Table of Contents

But the fruit of the Spirit is

LOVE, JOY, PEACE, LONGSUFFERING, GENTLENESS,

goodness, faith, meekness, temperance:

AGAINST SUCH THERE IS NO LAW.

GALATIANS 5:22, 23

And walk in *love,* as Christ also hath *loved* us, and hath given himself for us an *offering* and a *sacrifice* to God for a *sweetsmelling savour.*

Ephesians 5:2

Graciously

My "love" has limits:

   "All but *them*!"

   "Until *this* place!"

   "If *they* love me!"

       I hold my "love" in check until

       I find a cause that suits my will.

God's love is boundless:

   "Free to *all*!"

   "Beyond *this* place!"

   "I loved them *first*!"

       No holding back by what may be,

       He gives His love graciously.

one
The Fruit of the Spirit is

Love

SOME FARMERS GROW MORE THAN JUST ONE KIND OF fruit. An orchard may contain peach, apple, and pear trees. Grapefruit, orange, and persimmon might make up another. What a luscious variety!

Like an orchard of diversity, God grows in us a variety of spiritual fruits. All go toward the same purpose—to glorify God—yet each one is unique and important of itself.

The very first fruit of the Spirit mentioned is love. A vast word with a depth of meaning. Let's take a closer look.

In John 14:15, Jesus says, *If ye love me, keep my commandments.* And one of His commands is *love one another, as I have loved you* (John

15:12). As He loved us. How did Jesus love? Here is just a glimpse:

Sacrificially: *Hereby perceive we the love of God, because he laid down his life for us: and we ought to lay down our lives for the brethren* (I John 3:16).

Unconditionally: *But God commendeth his love toward us, in that, while we were yet sinners, Christ died for us* (Romans 5:8).

Steadfastly: *Having loved his own which were in the world, he loved them unto the end* (John 13:1).

How can we follow in Jesus' footsteps? Here are just a few suggestions from God's Word. (As we seek to live these things out, it helps to remember that *we* are not always so lovable ourselves.):

Sacrificially: Giving up our rights and comforts for the furtherance of the Gospel and the upbuilding of the body of Christ. Doing to others as we would have them do to us—even when it hurts. Bearing one another's burdens. Returning good for evil (II Tim. 4:5, Matt. 7:12, Gal. 6:2, Matt. 5:44).

Unconditionally: Extending forgiveness—even to those who don't ask for it. Having compassion on the unlovable. Seeking to pull sinners out of the fire (Eph. 4:32, Jude 22-23). Note in Jude 23 that this does not mean we love or condone *sin*.

Steadfastly: Living out the life of love to the very end—no matter how we feel, what others say, or how long the way may seem (I Cor. 15:58).

Can we love like Jesus? Not on our own! But as we yield to the Holy Spirit's work in us, He is able to change us more and more into Christ's image. Thank God for that. The place to start is by drawing near to the Lord and learning more about Him. The more we know Him, the more we love Him; and the more we love Him, the more we love *like* Him.

✱   ✱   ✱

Several months ago, God brought these truths home in a deep, personal way. I was dealing with a difficult situation, and found it hard to truly love those involved. So I asked God to help me grow. "Help me to love, Lord," I prayed. Yet I did not fully realize the difference between true and false love.

So He began to show me. The difficult situation I was going through came to a lull for awhile, and I began to grow confident (and maybe a bit prideful too). After all, I was doing pretty good. I found it easy to say the words, "I love you," and to feel a glow of tender affection. Love. Right?

Wrong! About that time, the difficult situation arose again. And, preoccupied with my attainments, I fell hard. "Lord, what happened?"

It seemed as if the Lord said to me then, "Child, true love is proved when tested. I said I loved you and I felt tender affection, but it didn't end there. I proved my love by dying on the cross for you—even while you were dead in your sins. Seek me anew for love like this."

Humbled and in awe, I went to my loving Lord and prayed a new prayer—one that went something like this: "Give me of Your genuine love, Lord, for all others are but a counterfeit!"

What About You?

Are you having a hard time loving someone? Look past the things you see, the hurts you feel, the unfairness you perceive, and remember that God loves you despite your sins against Him, your countless failures, and your often-cold heart. How can you withhold love when He gives so much?

Write out a prayer for a love like His. Then write at *least* one thing you can do today to *show* love to that hard-to-love one. Maybe it's as small as giving a kind reply or a gentle smile. Maybe it's something much, much bigger. Whatever it is, write it below and then do it!

_____

_____

_____

_____

_____

_____

_____

_____

_____

_____

Seeking Knowledge

Are you ready to dig deeper and reach higher after God's truths? What you need most of all is a Bible and a receptive heart. Then gather together a pen and a dictionary, and let's get started!

Find the Meaning: A study of *Strong's Concordance* reveals the fact that love is affection or benevolence, "embracing especially the judgment and *deliberate* assent of the will as a matter of principle, duty, and propriety."

So it isn't *just* feelings and words though those often do come into the picture. Look up the words *affection* and *benevolence* and write out the definition.

_____

_____

_____

Let the Light In: Psalm 119:130 tells us, *The entrance of thy words giveth light; it giveth understanding unto the simple.* Why not read I Corinthians 13 then write out:

• The things that are a dead and empty form (vv. 1-3).

_____

_____

_____

_____

- The characteristics of love (vv. 4-8).

_____

_____

_____

_____

_____

_____

_____

_____

_____

- The greatest of all things that abide (v. 13).

_____

_____

_____

Now take a moment to write out several ways in which God has specifically shown *you* these characteristics of love:

_____

_____

_____

_____

Adopt a Motto: To truly love, I must love like Jesus.

Do you want to read a heart-searching book on the topic of love? Then *If*, by Amy Carmichael, is just the one! (Christian Light Publications PO Box 1212, Harrisonburg, VA 22803-1212. Phone 540.434.0768.)

This book is a favorite of mine. I hope it will soon become a favorite of yours too.

Ponder a Prayer:
"Teach me thus Thy steps to trace,
Strong to follow in Thy grace,
Learning how to love from Thee,
Loving Him who first loved me."

Jane Eliza Leeson

Up to the *Brim*

The most joyous joy is empty
Where God is not.
Hollow, aching, not enough,
Though dearly bought.

But even simple joys will rise
Up to the brim,
Laden with a rich delight,
When God's in them.

Joy

ENVIRONMENT. HOW IMPORTANT TO AN ORCHARD! THE correct balance of sunshine, warmth, and humidity play an essential role in the ripening of fruit.

So what does it take to ripen the fruits of the Spirit? Nothing other than the environment of God's presence. We see this of joy in particular in Psalm 16:11: *Thou wilt shew me the path of life: in thy presence is fulness of joy; at thy right hand there are pleasures for evermore.*

What is this path of life? It's salvation through Christ, obedience to God's Word, and a life lived in the center of His will—whether that includes health or sickness, riches or poverty, singlehood or marriage, barrenness or motherhood, companionship with a husband or widowed and alone.

What is God calling us to as women? Whatever it is, if we obey His Word and follow the Holy Spirit's guidance, His presence will go with us. He will meet us there and surround us with the perfect balance of love and goodness, correction and instruction, provision and power. In this place we will experience joy—joy that's there because God is there, His way is best, His plan is perfect, and He knows what He's doing.

Is this the end? By all means, no. This beautiful path leads always higher, always onward, until we are finally brought home to heaven. And there we will experience the presence of God in full. We will stand at His right hand and look into His face without any veil of mortality or shadow of sin between. All will be swept entirely away, and perfect ripened joy will be ours.

Right now God says to each of us, "Child, I want to show you the path of life. My presence will walk with you, and this will be your joy. Take my hand and follow me."

And we say, "Yes, Lord, we will."

✳   ✳   ✳

It was a bright Sunday in October, and the sermon at church was on Psalm 100 (the passage that commands us to be thankful to God and bless His name). After the sermon, our pastor gave us this challenge: "Start a 'Thankfulness Book.' Every day write down one thing you are thankful for—making sure it differs from each previous entry. This is an exercise in proving the greatness of our good God."

Interesting idea! I went home and immediately took up the challenge. My first entry said, "Thank you for salvation." Later entries included things as simple as the colors of fall or a cup of hot tea, and as complex as perfection in Christ or having God as my Helper. I also included several pages of verses on being thankful to God—like Psalm 100:4, I Thess. 5:18, and Eph. 5:20.

Obeying God's command to give thanks took time and dedicated effort. But as I came into God's presence to focus on a new element of His goodness to me, guess what happened? You've got it! My joy began to ripen into a bountiful harvest. How could it be otherwise? His mercies are new every morning and His blessings are abundant. His joy is lasting because it is rooted in who He is, what He's done, and what He will do.

Why don't you try a "Thankfulness Book" too? "If you keep your eyes open, you can find new evidences of God's goodness in seemingly trivial events." Never will you exhaust His giving, nor the joy He has for you. Come. Step into His presence and give thanks!

What About You?

God wants to see His joy in you (see John 17:13). But you can only experience this as you live close to Him. Have you come into His presence through Christ? Are you abiding in Him by obedience, prayer in Jesus' name, and study of His Word? Ask God, for Christ's sake, to lead you onward in the path of life. Then make a schedule to pray and dig into God's Word every day. Here is a Bible study plan that has been helpful to me: Pick a book of the Bible. Read a small portion. Jot down, in a paragraph or less, one truth that impacts you. Then seek to live it out as you walk in joy-filled fellowship with God!

_____

_____

_____

_____

_____

_____

Seeking Knowledge

Glistening with beauty and delight, joy is a fruit we want to know more about. So let's start searching. And as we learn, let's remember to make our knowledge not just of the head, but also of the heart.

Find the Meaning: Look up the word *joy* and write out the definition.

_____

_____

_____

Let the Light In: Read John 14:6, 15:7, and 16:23-24.
• Who is my only access into the presence of the Father (14:6)?

_____

_____

_____

_____

• As I come to the Father through my access, with His Word abiding in me and my heart abiding in Him, what are the two results (15:7, 16:23-24)?

_____

_____

_____

_____

Now read Jude 24 and 25.
- What is God able to do for me (v. 24)?

_____

_____

_____

- What should my response be to my wonderful God (v. 25)?

_____

_____

_____

Finally, turn to Proverbs 14:13.
- List the two results of empty "joy" apart from God's presence.

_____

_____

_____

Adopt a Motto: The presence of God brings the presence of joy.

Ponder a Prayer:
"Be Thou my Sun, my selfishness destroy,
Thy atmosphere of Love be all my joy;
Thy Presence be my sunshine ever bright,
My soul the little mote that lives but in Thy light.

Gerhard Tersteegen

The Path of Trust

I have a choice:
  Will my today be filled with fear?
  Will I forget that God is near?
  Will I, within a gloomy way,
  Live all the moments of my day?

I have a choice:
  Oh, may I rise instead to live
  In all the peace that God can give,
  To walk the path of trust and be
  From gloomy fears at last set free!

three
The Fruit of the Spirit is

Peace

HOW WOULD YOU DESCRIBE A DILIGENT FRUIT FARMER? The best word that comes to mind is giving. From day one he unreservedly imparts careful planning and tedious toil. And the results? All is well in his orchard.

How like our dear Owner and Husbandman. *He that spared not his own Son, but delivered him up for us all, how shall he not with him also freely give us all things* (Romans 8:32)? From the plan of salvation all the way down to the minute details of everyday life, He gives abundantly.

Let's take a look at one of His great gifts: peace. In John 14:27, He says, *Peace I leave with you, my peace I give unto you: not as the world giveth, give I unto you. Let not your heart be troubled, neither let it be afraid.*

This peace is reconciliation with God, for our sins are washed away by Jesus' blood. It is concord with others, for He enables us to love our neighbor as ourselves. It is contentment with circumstances, for we are assured that He is working all things together for our good.

Truly, our God gives. Not as the world gives, with its unreliable, false securities, but with solid, long lasting peace. Right now He holds peace out to us and says, "Take. Do not be troubled or afraid. I have made provision for each one of your needs. Let my Spirit work the fruit of peace in you."

And as a yielded "orchard," we reply, "Lord, we trust You: the power of Your blood, the sufficiency of Your grace, and the wisdom of Your orchestration in each event of our lives."

Our God gives, we take, and all is well.

✻   ✻   ✻

Though peace is a gift freely given, there was a season in my life when I didn't quite know how to receive it. This season started when I was twelve years old and fear began to creep into my life. Fear. It's an ugly word that brings torment, and it gripped at my heart nearly every day. As soon as one fear left, another always came. And I, ignorant and gullible, fell for it every time.

At fifteen, fear had grown with my growth. It now held me captive. I remember crying out to God time and time again, "Lord, please deliver me!" Yet I didn't know exactly what was wrong.

Then at twenty-one, something clicked inside my mind: "I am listening to the voice of the enemy instead of the voice of God. God's Word says, 'Fear not. Trust in the Lord.' But Satan loves to persuade me to disobey. And I've been listening!"

So after years of torment, light began to dawn. God was answering my often-repeated prayer for deliverance. Now I knew that fear was disobedience to God, and that listening to God's voice—instead of the enemy's—was a choice that I had to make.

With God's help, I began to make that choice. I started saying an emphatic *No!* to the fearful suggestions of Satan and my tortured mind—and a resounding *Yes!* to the voice of God. The former brings panic and torment, the latter comfort and security.

As I placed my trust in God, something wonderful began to grow in me by the power of His Spirit—something I had honestly thought would never come my way: Peace! Oh Lord, how I praise You!

Now I stand as a testimony of God's delivering power. Oh, yes, I still struggle with fear on occasion, but it no longer rules my life. It doesn't have to rule yours either.

What About You?

What are you letting in that's robbing you of peace right now? A sin? A conflict? A fear? Search your heart and write out something specific. Then write a prayer of exchange: "Lord, here is my [sin, or conflict, or fear] for Your [cleansing blood, or harmony, or confidence]."

Later, when that sin tempts you, you will be hid in Jesus. When that conflict resurfaces, you will be enabled to treat others as you would like to have them treat you. When that fear brings torment, you will be quick to cast it upon God and go forth singing!

Seeking Knowledge

Life is full of fears, turmoils, tests, struggles, and strife, isn't it? Aren't you glad that we are not left in the midst of it all without a refuge? God is near, and He's holding out His arms for us to run unto Him. Let's come so we can take of His peace.

Find the Meaning: Look up the word *peace* and write out the definition.

_____

_____

_____

Let the Light In: Read James 1:17 and Colossians 3:15.
- Where does every good and perfect gift come from—including peace (James 1:17)?

_____

_____

_____

_____

- What makes these gifts so solid and reliable (James 1:17)?

_____

_____

_____

_____

• When God gives the gift of peace, what does He expect me to do with it (Colossians 3:15)?

_____

_____

_____

_____

Now turn to Isaiah 26:3 and Philippians 4:6-7.
• List some ways you can let peace rule (Isaiah 26:3, Philippians 4:6).

_____

_____

_____

_____

• List two characteristics of the peace God gives (Isaiah 26:3, Philippians 4:7).

_____

_____

_____

_____

• List the wonderful work it will accomplish in you (Philippians 4:7).

_____

_____

_____

_____

Adopt a Motto: God chose to give peace; I choose to take peace.

Ponder a Prayer:
"My heart is resting, O my God,
I will give thanks and sing;
My heart is at the secret source
Of every precious thing.

Chorus:
O peace of God that passeth thought,
I daily, hourly sing,
My heart is at the secret source
Of every precious thing."

Anna L Waring

Peace I leave with you,
my peace I give unto you:
not as the world giveth,
give I unto you.
Let not your heart be troubled,
neither let it be afraid.

John 14:27

A BLEND OF
Beauty

To suffer long. This fruit in me
Combines in perfect harmony
   The patience of forbearance and
   The strength of fortitude to stand.

It touches every faze of strife—
Inside and out of all my life.
   It leaves its mark upon the way—
A blend of beauty every day.

four
The Fruit of the Spirit is
Longsuffering

THINK OF THE UNIQUE COMPLEXITY OF AN APPLE. There's the smooth, shiny skin on the outside; the crisp, juicy flesh beneath; and a hard, seed-filled core. An apple isn't made up of a single dimension.

Longsuffering is a lot like that. First it consists of forbearance toward others, and then fortitude in the face of trials. It's two-fold. A spiritual fruit with two important aspects.

Aspect #1: The ability to stay unruffled by sharp or untrue words, misjudgments, and unkind actions. As the Holy Spirit cultivates this in my life, I can say, "This wrong done by another is in God's hands. I do not need to retaliate, vindicate myself, or prove who's right. I am at peace in the patience only God can give." And longsuffering blossoms and sets fruit.

Aspect #2: The ability to remain calm and quiet when subjected to hindering circumstances, deep pain, unfulfilled desires, and prolonged affliction. Here again it takes the work of the Holy Spirit to help me say, "In this trial, have Your way, Lord. Be the time long or short, I wait Your will. I choose to let patience have her perfect work" (see James 1:2-4). Now the fruit of longsuffering begins to ripen.

Just as this fruit contains two spiritual characteristics, it also offers two-fold blessings: Serenity and sufficient grace straight from the hand of God. Both come down to lift us above the pain of adversity and trial. Do we want these blessings? It's time we yield to God's Spirit, allowing Him to grow the fruit!

✳   ✳   ✳

I've had many opportunities to practice the two-fold aspects of longsuffering. Many of those instances resulted in nothing more than shameful failure and a flying to God for forgiveness. But others, though mixed with failure, have ended victoriously because I allowed God to have His way with me. May I share two of those triumphs with you?

Forbearance: Someone said something hurtful to me. A deep desire welled up inside to say something hurtful back. But then God began to speak softly into my heart: "Child, take the truth from their words and use them to help you grow. Then let the rest go. Be silent. Be patient. Be humble."

"Okay, Lord, I'll follow Your way." With those words I discovered the power to go forward in silence and serenity.

Fortitude: "Oh Lord, please make this stop right now!" That was the cry of my heart as I faced a seemingly unbearable trial several years ago. When God didn't answer as I thought He should, I wallowed in agonizing tears, excruciating inner struggles, and deep depression. How long did this have to go on, anyway?

"God, You are so powerful that You could put an end to this problem right away," I cried. "Why don't You?"

Now I praise God that He didn't. He had an eternal purpose for letting the trial linger. Reaching the end of myself, I fell battered and broken into His arms. And it was there that I learned to wait, to trust, and to go forward in strength, despite the pain. I realized His grace is sufficient and His love unbounded.

I think you'll agree with me that it was worth the wait!

What About You?

Has someone tested your patience? Is a trial lingering long? Write out a prayer of commitment to walk in two-fold longsuffering—no matter what. Then jot down some eternal purposes you see God working in you through this problem. Compassion toward others? A deeper reliance on God? The realization that the Lord is all-perceiving, and therefore knows what He's doing?

Okay. Now start walking! Remain silent when words of retaliation arise. Praise God in your fiery trial. And use the lessons you are learning to help someone else. You aren't the only one struggling to walk worthy of your vocation.

_____

_____

_____

_____

_____

Seeking Knowledge

I'm excited to go one step further by delving into the value of a long-suffering spirit. Want to join me?

Find the Meaning: Look up the word *longsuffering* and write out the definition.

_____

_____

_____

Let the Light In: Forbearance: Read Ephesians 3:14-21 and 4:1-3.
• What six things does the Father grant to me (3:14-19)?

_____

_____

_____

• To whom belongs the glory forever (3:20-21)?

_____

_____

_____

_____

• What am I beseeched to do in this vocation wherein I am called (4:1)?

_____

_____

_____

_____

• What five things should mark my walk (4:2-3)?

_____

_____

_____

_____

_____

Fortitude: Read Colossians 1:9-11. There it is again—that "walk worthy" exhortation! (see v. 10).

• What does this "walking worthy" include (v. 10)?

_____

_____

_____

_____

• What is the source of my strength to follow this command (v. 11)?

_____

_____

_____

_____

- What needs to go along with my patience and longsuffering (v. 11)?

_____

_____

_____

_____

Now turn to Isaiah 30:18.
- Why does the Lord sometimes wait to end a trial or grant a request?

_____

_____

_____

_____

- What is the result of my patiently waiting on Him?

_____

_____

_____

_____

Adopt a Motto: To walk in longsuffering is to walk in blessings.

Ponder a Prayer:
"Breathe on me, Breath of God,
Until my heart is pure,
Until with Thee I will one will—
To do and to endure."

Edwin Hatch

And the servant of the Lord must not strive; but be gentle unto all men, apt to teach, patient.
II Timothy 2:24

Reality

You may stand tall in your own eyes
And think that you are very wise,
  Yet do you have this little thing:
  The gentleness true wisdom brings?

For if the answer is a *No*,
Reality will surely show
  The "wisdom" that you think you see
  Is but an ugly fallacy.

five

The Fruit of the Spirit is

Gentleness

THE ORCHARD LIES IN A TWILIGHT HUSH. ONLY THE soft rustle of leaves and the gentle cooing of a dove breaks the silence. Suddenly a stealthy figure slinks among the trees. Unmindful of torn branches and trampled grass, his hands quickly pluck fruit and shove it into a bag. Thief! He comes to steal, kill, and destroy.

But when the owner comes, things are different. He moves among his trees with a confident step, carefully encouraging growth and plucking fruit. He comes to give life.

In the orchard of our spiritual lives, Satan's purpose is that of the thief. In James 3, we see how his hands seek to steal and destroy the lovely fruit of gentleness: *But if ye have bitter envying and strife in your hearts, glory not, and lie not against the truth. This wisdom descendeth not from above, but is earthly, sensual, devilish. For where envying and strife is, there is confusion and every evil work* (vv. 14-16). What destruction! How can gentleness survive when trampled and plucked by the workings of satanic wisdom?

But look! Here comes our Owner with His life-giving presence. He says, *But the wisdom that is from above is first pure, then peaceable, gentle, and easy to be intreated, full of mercy and good fruits, without partiality, and without hypocrisy* (James 3:17).

Next time Satan slinks into our orchards with his destructive wisdom like, "I want that!" "Me first!" "It isn't fair!" "Stay out of my way!" or "I'll get even!" let's call on our Owner. He will come quickly and put an end to such thievery. His Spirit will whisper to us, "Let me give," "You first," "I'm glad for them," "How can I help?" "I'll turn the other cheek."

No thief can stay when the Owner is near!

✻   ✻   ✻

One evening, not too long ago, I came face-to-face with the enemy's sneaky maneuvers to rob me of gentleness. The evening began with me making a plan for my precious spare moments—a plan that looked something like this:

- Do a little work on my newest writing project.
- Have my evening devotions.
- Go to bed early.

It didn't work. Instead someone in my family wanted to stay up late and talk. Harsh feelings arose, irritated words came out, and my attitude said, "I don't have time for you!"

Later I evaluated my reaction. Gentle? W-e-l-l. Not really. So I asked the Lord, "Please make me gentle. Impart Your wisdom so I can know how to handle the breaking in upon my schedule. Which situations require a firm yet gentle, "I have something I need to do," and which ones call for a dropping of all plans to listen and help?

Usually the answer is obvious—if I just let God speak. One thing always stands clear in the light of His wisdom: *No* situation ever calls for harsh and selfish actions. Never.

From now on, when my schedule lies in shambles at my feet, I want to see that gentleness stays intact. May it look something like this:

- Considerate of others' feelings.
- Gracious in expression and tone.
- Generous in the giving of my time.

What About You?

Write out a sincere, faith-filled prayer for wisdom from above. Then let God reveal to you any lack of gentleness in your life. Is He showing you some ugly things, like He's shown me? Don't shrink away. Allow the Holy Spirit to prune those unsightly, damaging branches, and let Him purify you.

Now stop and consider how gentleness would react in the areas where you are not gentle. For instance, maybe the Lord has revealed to you a habit of making sarcastic remarks. Gentleness would say sweet words that fall like a balm. Write that down, and then go and *say* those words!

_____

_____

_____

_____

_____

_____

Seeking Knowledge

Our Father knows what we have need of before we even ask (Matthew 6:8). The fact that gentleness is a foreign element to our nature is no surprise to Him! As He cultivates the heart, He alone ignites the spark of desire to have this fruit. And He wants us to yield to Him as He works it in us. Praise Him for that!

Find the Meaning: Look up the word *gentle* and write out the definition.

_____

_____

_____

Let the Light In: Read Daniel 2:20 and James 1:5-7 for a look at wisdom from above.

• Who does true wisdom belong to (Daniel 2:20)?

_____

_____

_____

_____

• What is the logical action I should take when I need wisdom (James 1:5)?

_____

_____

_____

_____

• What is the result of this action, when done in faith (James 1:5-7)?

_____

_____

_____

_____

• What does God give (James 1:5)?

_____

_____

_____

_____

Now read II Timothy 2:23-26 for a look at the marks of satanic "wisdom" and true wisdom.

• What genders strife (v. 23)?

_____

_____

_____

_____

• As servants of God, what must I do and *not* do (v. 24)?

_____

_____

_____

_____

• Who am I to be gentle to (v. 24)?

_____

_____

_____

_____

Adopt a Motto: Would I be wise? Let me be gentle. Would I be gentle? Let me be wise.

Ponder a Prayer:
"Gracious Spirit, dwell with me;
I myself would gracious be;
And with words that help and heal
Would Thy life in mine reveal."

Thomas Toke Lynch

Finally, my brethren, be strong in the Lord, and in the power of his might.

Ephesians 6:10

Prepared

II Timothy 2:21

I want this word to be
Descriptive, Lord, of me:
Prepared!

To stand in purity
And know You've fitted me
To give.

The good planned out by You
I want to go and do—
Prepared!

Goodness

DISEASED, BUG-INFESTED, ROTTED. TREES LIKE THAT are not going to bear fruit. *Useless* is their lot, and eventually they will have to be cut down. What a sad plight for the trees. What a disappointment to the husbandman!

But listen to this: In our spiritual orchard, we have a Husbandman who can actually *restore*. To heal, purify, and strengthen are all within His power.

As we already know, the starting point to this restoration is Christ's blood, which purges the disease of our sin and covers us with His spotless righteousness. Then it moves on to a daily, hourly sanctification by His Spirit—which prunes the infestation of bad habits and besetting sins. Faithfully God works on us until we stand strong and sound in Him. And the result? The glorious fruit of goodness.

First, we are enabled to live a life of purity, which means saying *No* to that which taints, and *Yes* to that which pleases God. It means coming regularly in repentance to the mercy seat. It means walking in an upright and honest way.

Second, we are enabled to live a life that reaches out to help others. This means sharing the Gospel, lending a helping hand, giving to the poor, visiting the fatherless and widows. The list can go on and on as we seek to bring souls to God and bear one another's burdens.

Stop for a moment and think about it: Through God's power, we are no longer useless trees destined to die. As we allow God to work in us, no sharp ax will ever come to chop us down. Instead, we are destined to grow larger, stronger, and more productive with the passing of each new day. Now that's a marvel.

✳   ✳   ✳

I am so thankful for the transforming work of God. The truth is that, in my natural human state, I couldn't care less about helping others. My focus was all about me and what others could do for me.

Things changed when God made me a new creation. I began to ask, "What can I do to reach out to others, God? What can I do to point them to You and make their pathway brighter?"

God had several specific answers for me, including: "Use your pen."

I hesitated. "Really, God? Can someone like me actually help people in that way?"

The answer was, "No. But I can work through you." And that's all I needed to know!

Letting the goodness of God flow through me isn't always an easy thing, though. Selfishness still infests me at times, and I have to run to

God for restoration. But this just makes me praise Him more, for I realize that all the good I do comes *only* from Him. Have I touched a heart and eased its pain? It is Him! Have I reached out and cheered a fellow pilgrim fainting on the way? It is Him! Have I pointed someone to the Savior's wounded side? It is Him!

As saved ones, God has a ministry He's calling each one of us to fulfill. We should stop focusing on our weakness, and start trusting in His sufficient grace. It's all we need.

What About You?

Is your spiritual life slowly being eaten away by the infestation of sin? Run to God. Let Him restore you.

Are your goals for goodness all out of whack? Realign them to the goal *God* has set.

Are you ready to walk down the path of goodness? Write some specific ways in which you can say *No* to *your* besetting sin and *Yes* to God.

_____

_____

_____

Now start thinking about ministry. Do you know what God is calling you to do in this season of your life? With an open heart, seek His face about this. Then write down what He reveals. How can you prepare for it? How can you set about to *do* it?

_____

_____

_____

_____

Seeking Knowledge

As we do our study on this particular fruit, it is important to remember the purpose of goodness. It is not to gain salvation, rack up points, or get pats on the back. Our goodness comes from God, and is therefore not ours at all. Rather, it is a gift He commands us to cherish and cultivate. Let's take a closer look at the *how*, the *why*, and the *way* of goodness.

Find the Meaning: Look up the word *good* and write out the definition.

_____

_____

_____

Let the Light In: Read Psalm 23:3.
How: • What comes first before I am led into righteousness?

_____

_____

_____

Now read Matthew 5:16.
Why: • What is the purpose of letting my light shine?

_____

_____

_____

Finally read Titus 2:14, Micah 6:8, James 1:27, and James 4:17.

Way: • What marks me as one redeemed and purified by God (Titus 2:14)?

_____

_____

_____

• What does the Lord require of me (Micah 6:8)?

_____

_____

_____

• What characterizes pure and undefiled religion (James 1:27)?

_____

_____

_____

• What is the weight of my responsibility (James 4:17)?

_____

_____

_____

Adopt a Motto: As God pours goodness in, I cannot help but pour goodness out.

Ponder a Prayer:
"How I praise Thee, precious Savior,
That Thy love laid hold of me;
Thou hast saved and cleansed and filled me
That I might Thy channel be."

Mary E. Maxwell

Trustworthy One

MARK 4:35-40

A slash of wind,

A dash of spray,

  A storm upon the deep.

      And, Lord, it seems You do not care

      Nor heed the cry of my despair.

A Power great,

A Love divine,

  A Voice that is obeyed.

      Lord, how could I have doubted You?

      Trustworthy One, faithful and true!

seven

The Fruit of the Spirit is

Faith

CONSIDER AN ORCHARD IN THE GRIP OF A FIERCE storm. Dark clouds blot out the sun. Cold rain pelts down. Strong wind tears through the trees. It seems impossible that the sun will ever shine, or that calm will ever settle over the orchard. Yet storms must lift, and peace surely comes. This is but a time for roots to seek a firmer hold within the soil, making for stronger trees and more abundant fruit.

Is our spiritual orchard in the grip of a difficult time right now? Perhaps the clouds of fear are blotting out hope, the rain of trials is pelting against us, and the wind of doubt is tossing to and fro. We do not have to despair. God wants to use this time to root us deeper in Him. As we cling to Him and His promises, His Spirit will produce the fruit of faith in us—faith grounded in an unalterable certainty: the faithfulness of God.

When He says salvation is in Jesus alone, or that He won't cast us out if we come to Him, or that He will never leave us nor forsake us (see Acts 4:12, John 6:37, Hebrews 13:5), we can believe Him. *He is faithful that promised* and *There hath not failed one word of all his good promise, which he promised* (Hebrews 10:23 and I Kings 8:56). His character is beyond reproach.

Look past the doubts and difficulties and cling to God. Allow His Spirit to work the faith in us to say, "Lord, '[we] believe [You], that it shall be even as it was told [us]' (Acts 27:25). Come walk us through this difficult storm in our lives and bring us on to a deeper establishment. We stake everything on You!"

✳   ✳   ✳

Just today I experienced a testing of my faith. Everything seemed to be going wrong, and doubt hovered on the horizon. "Lord, where are You? Do You care? Why are You allowing this?"

Not wanting to succumb to these ugly questions, I got out my Bible, lifted up a prayer for faith, and began to search God's promises. Here's what I found to combat each one of my doubts:

Where are You? *Lo, I am with you always, even unto the end of the world* (Matthew 28:20).

Do You care? *Casting all your care upon him; for he careth for you* (I Peter 5:7).

Why are You allowing this? *For I know the thoughts that I think toward you, saith the Lord, thoughts of peace, and not of evil, to give you an expected end* (Jeremiah 29:11).

As I clung to God's Word, faith sprang up in me and doubt faded away. My God is faithful. I am never alone or uncared for. All of my life is planned—even a day like this one is—a day where I can't get much done, problems arise that I don't know how to solve, and tension fills me until I am afraid I will explode.

And you know what? I'm actually beginning to see a purpose in today already. When life is not lovely, God's promises glow with an added luster. Today they become exceedingly precious to me. And grasped by faith, they turned my unlovely day into a thing of beauty!

God's promises can do the same for anyone!

What About You?

Are you held in the grip of a hardship right now? Maybe it's the death of a loved one, the severing of a friendship, or the withering of a dream. Whatever it is, ask God to increase your faith in this dark time (see Luke 17:5). Then get into His Word. What promise is He holding out to you in this particular situation? What does this promise reveal about His character? Write it down, and then stake your all on Him!

_____

_____

_____

_____

_____

_____

Seeking Knowledge

Faith in God: who He is, what He has done, what He is doing, and what He will do. As children of God, trusting in Jesus Christ for salvation, we have the fundamentals of faith. But there are still areas in our lives where doubt and unbelief linger. By God's power, let's seek to grow past these doubts until the fruit of faith is made evident in our lives!

Find the Meaning: Look up the word *faith* and write out the definition.

_____

_____

_____

Let the Light In: Read Psalm 36:5, Psalm 89:1, and II Timothy 2:13.
• What is the scope of God's faithfulness (Ps. 36:5, 89:1)?

_____

_____

_____

_____

• Why does doubt on my part utterly fail to shake God's faithfulness (II Tim. 2:13)?

_____

_____

_____

_____

Now read Hebrews 11:1, Romans 10:17, and Mark 9:24
- What is faith (Heb. 11:1)?

_____

_____

_____

_____

- Why is it so important to hear God's promises (Romans 10:17)?

_____

_____

_____

_____

- What should my prayer be (Mark 9:24)?

_____

_____

_____

_____

Adopt a Motto: My faith is grounded in God's faithfulness.

Ponder a Prayer:
"Help me then in every tribulation
So to trust Thy promises, O Lord,
That I lose not faith's sweet consolation
Offered me within Thy holy Word."

Lina Sandell Berg

Transformed!

ROMANS 12:2

To the world I stood conformed:

    Pressed in its mold,

    Stuck in its hold,

        Restricted by its prideful way.

        Yet thanks to God, I now can say:

In Him I stand transformed!

    Renewed in mind,

    My soul can find

        The freedom to let go of pride

        And walk in meekness by Christ's side.

eight
The Fruit of the Spirit is
Meekness

WORM-INFESTED FRUIT ISN'T ALWAYS EVIDENT. TO A casual onlooker, all may appear well. But the farmer knows. He inspects his fruit regularly and sees the worm holes. He understands the results: decay to his fruit.

When the fruit of meekness is being infested by pride, our Husbandman knows the signs too: boasting, condescension, faultfinding, arrogance, conceit, retaliation. For a time these signs may appear small. In fact, a facade of flawlessness can even hide from *ourselves* what is truly going on inside! Yet meekness is slowly being eaten away, and the fruit *will fall*!

But why let this destruction go on? God has a pesticide that can destroy pride and cause meekness to flourish. It's humility. He tells us, *Humble yourselves therefore under the mighty hand of God, that he may exalt you in due time* (I Peter 5:6).

That's where true meekness starts. One sincere look at Jesus' nail-scarred hands, and pride is stripped away. We see ourselves for what we really are: undone, vile, and desperately in need of a Savior. We realize that it is our sin that put Christ on the cross. We are nothing but death-worthy. Then we see in a new light His depth of mercy, His abundance of grace, and His mind of meekness that endured the cross of shame for us.

Out of that life-look, God's Spirit lifts us up to glory in nothing but the cross of Jesus Christ, for all our accomplishments are from Him. We are also enabled to treat all as equally worthy of our attention—for He died for everyone—to overlook others' faults—for we are no better than they—and to give up defending our rights—for God is our defense.

Where is pride now? It is gone. Meekness is left to grow unhindered.

* * *

Deep inside I long for meekness. But pride is a sneaky thing. For instance, have you ever been proud of *not* being proud? I have. In fact, God is revealing a little of that in my heart right now. My thoughts are saying: "Pride is such an awful thing. How can people harbor it? I'm glad *I* don't."

Oh, really? God is telling me otherwise. He says, "Look again, Child. I'm seeing more than meets your eye."

So I look again. "Oh Lord, how terrible!" I cry. "Now I see that I'm acting like the self-exalting Pharisee in Luke 18. His pride left him unjustified, empty, and deceived. Please deliver me from such a fate!"

God loves to answer a plea for help. I find Him drawing near, encouraging me to be like the self-denouncing publican who cried, *God be merciful to me a sinner* (Luke 18:13). He allowed God to transform his mind until he was utterly nothing in his own sight, yet fully confident of God's mercy.

So now my thoughts are taking a different direction as God works in me. I would no longer glory in myself. Rather I want to learn meekness at the mercy seat, where Christ intercedes for me. Then I will encounter (along with the publican of Luke 18) the glorious paradox of God's grace: I am sinful, yet justified; humbled, yet exalted; empty, yet thoroughly satisfied in God.

The publican, you, and I—may each of us have a personal experience in the paradox of grace.

What About You?

Right now take the time to let God renew your mind with meekness. Sit at Jesus' feet and ponder His work at Calvary. Then write out a prayer of self-denouncement and God-exaltation.

Then live in meekness. You can experience compassion rather than condemnation when you see someone who doesn't measure up by thinking— "There, but for the grace of God, go I." You can glory in the cross of Christ by sharing your testimony. You can esteem others better than yourself by respecting their opinions. You can give up strife by remaining silent when you want to defend yourself. With God's power transforming you, the list can go on and on!

_____

_____

_____

_____

_____

Seeking Knowledge

Stop and think about it. Though one with God and free from all sin, Jesus' entire walk on earth was characterized by meekness. How much more ought we to be meek—we who are nothing more than sinners saved by grace?

In Matthew 11:29, Jesus says, *Take my yoke upon you, and learn of me; for I am meek and lowly in heart: and ye shall find rest unto your souls.* Come. Let us subject ourselves to Christ and learn His meekness. Soul-rest will be the sure result.

Find the Meaning: Look up the word *meek* and write out the definition.

_____

_____

_____

_____

_____

Let the Light In: Read Philippians 2:1-11.
• What was Jesus' standing *before* He came to earth (v. 6)?

_____

_____

_____

_____

_____

• What five ways did He show meekness *when* He came to earth (vv. 7-8)?

_____

_____

_____

_____

_____

• What is His state *now* that He has fulfilled His mission on earth (vv. 9-11)?

_____

_____

_____

_____

_____

Jesus humbled Himself for us!
• How can I let His mind of meekness be seen (vv. 2-4)?

_____

_____

_____

_____

_____

Now turn to Romans 8:6.
- What is the result of the carnal mind (of which pride is a part of)?

_____

_____

_____

_____

_____

- What is the result of the spiritual mind (of which meekness is a part of)?

_____

_____

_____

_____

_____

Adopt a Motto: The exchange: my mind of pride for Christ's mind of meekness.

Ponder a Prayer:
"Plant in us an humble mind,
Patient, pitiful, and kind;
Meek and lowly let us be,
Full of goodness, full of Thee."

Charles Wesley

PUT ON THEREFORE,
as the elect of God,
HOLY AND BELOVED,
bowels of mercies,
KINDNESS,
humbleness of mind,
MEEKNESS,
longsuffering.
Colossians 3:12

This HiddenSnare

"I only self-indulge a bit.
   It doesn't really matter.
      There is no chance that it can bring
      A bit of harm—this little thing!"

Oh, subtle lie—this hidden snare!
   It works a world of havoc.
      To listen is to take the bait
      And face destruction as our fate.

nine

The Fruit of the Spirit is

Temperance

STAND BACK FOR A MOMENT AND LOOK AT AN ORCHARD left to run wild. Dead branches and deformed fruit hang from the trees. Tall weeds grow in matted tangles. The soil is hard and dry. Broken fence rails lay in shambles. What a sorry sight!

Now look at the exquisite order of an orchard brought into subjection. The trees are wisely pruned. Healthy fruit flourishes. The weeds are removed. The soil is cultivated and the trees are properly watered. The fences are sturdy. Now that's a lovely sight!

How is it with our spiritual orchard? When we give free reign to the indulgence of our carnal feelings and desires, self-destruction is the sure result. Are you willing to let this happen?

In the face of such a decision, God is holding out to us the only life-giving option. He says, *Let not sin therefore reign in your mortal body, that ye should obey it in the lusts thereof.* Instead, *Submit yourselves therefore to [me]* and say, *Not as I will, but as thou wilt* (see Romans 6:12, James 4:7, and Matthew 26:39).

To bring our lives into subjection to God's will is to see the fruit of temperance grow. By the power of the Holy Spirit, we are enabled to restrain our natural inclination toward sin, to practice moderation in even good things, and to bring every thought captive to the obedience of Christ (see II Corinthians 10:5). And the sure result? Exquisite order, of course.

※   ※   ※

I'm sorry to say that my life isn't in very exquisite order right now. It's all because of a God-honoring desire that I'm failing to bring into subjection to God's will. Yes, my desire is in accordance to the standards laid out in the Bible, and the realization of it is often granted to other people. Yet for some reason God hasn't seen fit to fulfill this desire for *me*. Standing here empty-handed I wonder why. And as I wonder, I let my emotions run wild in several different phases.

Phase #1: Soon—any time now!—circumstances will fall into place and I will experience the fulfillment of my desire.

Phase #2: Things aren't working out as I had planned—and maybe they never will.

Phase #3: What can I do to *make* my desire come true?

Battered and broken, I lift empty hands and cry, "God, why don't You just give me what I want?"

God's answer? *For my thoughts are not your thoughts, neither are your ways my ways... As the heavens are higher than the earth, so are my ways higher than your ways, and my thoughts than your thoughts. I know the thoughts that I think toward you...thoughts of peace, and not of evil, to give you an expected end. Be in subjection unto the Father of spirits, and live* (see Isaiah 55:8-9, Jeremiah 29:11, and Hebrews 12:9).

Humbled, awed, contrite, I gather up the varied emotions that run rampant. I hand them over to God.

"Dear Lord," I pray, "help me bring these emotions into a place of restraint. May I say with a controlled and quiet trust, 'Whatever You choose, Lord; whatever You choose.'"

Coming to this place, I am enabled to stand strong and stable, instead of battered and broken. It's a beautiful place to be!

What About You?

In what area do you find yourself carnally indulging? (Be aware that the devil will often try to sidetrack us into pointing the finger at others whose sins seem worse than our own. But this is useless.) Earnestly search your own heart for the sin that lurks there. Is it thoughts, words, appetites, or actions? Come in repentance to God and write out a "not as I will, but as Thou wilt" type of prayer. Then find a Bible verse that speaks about restraining your personal area of weakness and sin. How does it convict, challenge, and help you? How does putting it into practice bring order out of disorder? Try to write this last one down out of active experience, not just head knowledge.

_____

_____

_____

_____

_____

_____

Seeking Knowledge

Self-indulgence is often looked upon as freedom. And we all want to be free, right? Well, think again on what freedom really means. Self-indulgence only brings a bondage of destruction. Liberty is found in the will of God alone. Let that will bring our inclinations into order, and we are sure to discover a bursting of every bond. Our God delivers the captives!

Find the Meaning: Look up the word *temperance* and write out the definition.

_____

_____

_____

Let the Light In: Read Proverbs 25:28 and Romans 14:21. If you lack self-control:

• What am I likened to (Proverbs 25:28)?

_____

_____

_____

_____

• What do I cause in others (Romans 14:21)?

_____

_____

_____

_____

Now read Isaiah 61:1, Luke 4:18-19, Luke 21:34, I Corinthians 9:27, Philippians 2:13, and James 1:25.

- How does God make order out of chaos (Isaiah 61:1, Luke 4:18-19)?

_____

_____

_____

_____

- What is my warning (Luke 21:34)?

_____

_____

_____

_____

- What is my responsibility (I Corinthians 9:27)?

_____

_____

_____

_____

- Where is my power (Philippians 2:13)?

_____

_____

_____

_____

- What is my reward (James 1:25)?

_____

_____

_____

_____

Adopt a Motto: Temperance: a life of order ordered by God.

Ponder a Prayer:
"Oh, let my thought, my actions, and my will
Obedient solely to Thy impulse move,
My heart and senses keep Thou blameless still,
Fixed and absorbed in Thine unbounded love.
Thy praying, teaching, striving, in my heart,
Let me not quench, nor make Thee to depart.

Gerhard Tersteegen

And beside this, giving

all diligence, add

to your faith virtue;

and to virtue knowledge; And to knowledge

temperance; and to temperance patience; and to

patience godliness; And to godliness brotherly

kindness; and to brotherly kindness charity. For if

these things be in you, and abound, they make you

that ye shall neither be barren nor unfruitful in the

knowledge of our Lord Jesus Christ.

II Peter 1:5-8

Set *On* You

Fix my focus, Eternal One.
  The pull of earth is drawing.
    One fatal look and I
    Will see my life-work die.

Fix my focus, Eternal One,
  With pull of greater power.
    Once set my eyes alone on You,
    And I enduring work will do.

ten

Eternal Results

THE ONE *PURPOSE* OF AN ORCHARD IS TO PRODUCE FRUIT for its owner. And yet out of that one purpose can come multiple results. The fruit can be baked into pies and pastries, made into jellies and jams, or eaten fresh. The goodness of the fruit brings added health to the consumer, as well as delight to the taste buds.

So what about us? We already know what our one grand purpose is: to bring forth fruit for God's glory. But what are the *results* of this purpose? Here's a glimpse:

• We are brought closer to God. The more we yield to the work of the Holy Spirit, the more we are drawn to God. It's like the outgoing tide: throw yourself in, and you will be swept away to deeper depths of the ocean.

- We experience true fulfillment. Doing what God created and designed us to do brings satisfaction. It's like a potter's vessel shaped for use, and then filled to the brim.
- We point others to God. Transformed by the glory of His power, our lives will be like a beacon in the night. And those who are seeking will want to trace that light back to its Source.

Fellowship with God, spiritual satisfaction, and souls saved. What beautiful results that will not fade nor pass away! But how do we know that they will endure? For this express reason: they are not the temporal works of *our* finite hands. Rather, they are brought about by the touch of *God's* infinite Hand. And whatever He accomplishes will abide forever!

✳   ✳   ✳

Knowing these facts about eternal results should bring a restful quiet to my soul—no matter how long it takes to actually *see* the results. But unfortunately I'm not a very patient person. Being the type who wants to see things right away, I often wonder, "Why this sitting here in the dark? I want to know what's going on!"

Right now I'm impatient about my writing endeavors. How is God's power being used through the words He gives? Is my simple pen doing enough for His glory? Who is being pointed to Him as I strive (and often fail!) to let His fruit flourish in me?

But usually I don't get specific answers. Instead, it seems like God often says, "Wait awhile. You don't need to know yet." So I'm left sitting here in the dark, as my writing goes out beyond my vision. And I'm not alone! I've read from other authors who experience this same situation. Why is this so?

Perhaps it's to act as a reminder. Results aren't mine at all—they're God's. Because I am merely His tool, He has all authority. He can do as He wants, when He wants, and to reach whom He wants—without ever having to consult with me. He doesn't have to let me know what's going on until His appointed time.

But He never leaves me in the dark without something to hang on to. As I sit here, He gives me this joint admonition and assurance: *Therefore, my beloved brethren, be ye stedfast, unmoveable, always abounding in the work of the Lord, forasmuch as ye know that your labour is not in vain in the Lord* (I Corinthians 15:58). Whatever He accomplishes through me will not be in vain. One day He will let me see it all, and not one particle will be lost. Can't the seeing wait?

What About You?

Take a moment to evaluate your focus. Maybe you are straining to see immediate results, like I've shared about myself. Look up to the One who controls all. Write out a prayer for patience, saying, "Lord, I commit my way to You. I trust also in You, knowing You will bring it to pass" (see Psalm 37:5).

Or maybe your eyes are fixed on earthly things that will fade away. Ask God to rivet your eyes on Him—the Eternal One—so that He can continue to work through you.

Next step? Write out a list of ways you can keep your focus where it belongs. Memorizing Scriptures and praying regularly should get you started. Now go put your list into practice.

_____

_____

_____

_____

_____

Eternal. How can our finite minds fully grasp such a concept? They can't! But what they *can* understand will change our focus forever. Let's seek to gain that understanding.

Find the Meaning: **Look up the word *eternal* and write out the definition.**

_____

_____

_____

Let the Light In: **Read Psalm 102:25-26, Luke 12:19-20, and I Peter 1:24.**
- Make a list of some of the passing things of this world.

_____

_____

_____

Look at Psalm 102:26-27, I Peter 1:25, Psalm 145:13, John 10:28, and I Timothy 6:16.
- List who is eternal and what is eternal through Him.

_____

_____

_____

_____

• List the descriptions of this eternity.

_____

_____

_____

_____

Now turn to Hebrews 12:2, II Corinthians 4:18, and I Corinthians 3:1-15.

• *Who* should my focus be riveted on (Hebrews 12:2)?

_____

_____

_____

_____

• *What* should my focus be riveted to (II Corinthians 4:18)?

_____

_____

_____

• What will happen to all temporal work (I Corinthians 3:15)?

_____

_____

_____

_____

- What will happen to all work done with the eternal God (I Corinthians 3:14a)?

_____

_____

_____

_____

Adopt a Motto: The eternal God brings about eternal results.

Ponder a Prayer:

"Firm against every doubt of Thee
For all my future way—
To walk in heaven's eternal light
Throughout the changing day.
Ah! such a day as Thou shalt own
When suns have ceased to shine!
A day of burdens borne by Thee,
And work that all was Thine."

Anna L. Waring

For the wages of sin is death; but the gift of God is eternal life through Jesus Christ our Lord.

Romans 6:23

The *Now*

This growing season is not forever.

Lord, I am glad.

I know that this hard way

Leads to a perfect day.

Yet what about the *now* that I must face?

Lord, You are here!

This lends a glory to

Each stage I'm walking through.

eleven

Beauty in the Process

WHEN A HUSBANDMAN STANDS AND SURVEYS HIS flourishing groves, he knows the process behind it. Those gnarled, fruit-laden trees had quite a humble beginning: just latent seeds pushed into soil! Slowly they turned into tiny sprouts, then spindly saplings, then half-grown trees, until finally they reached the place where they are now. Yet in each stage the farmer saw beauty and purpose. Why? Because he knew the potential.

If we are honest with ourselves, none of us will dare to claim perfect establishment. A survey of our hearts and lives will immediately reveal plenty of room to grow. And this knowledge can turn us to despair. How far we have to go. How pitifully immature we are.

But, oh! we do not need to be discouraged! We have a Husbandman who delights in our growth process. When we become a Christian, when we gain a deeper knowledge of God, when we win a victory, when we begin to produce a spiritual fruit—*each* tiny step, no matter how seemingly imperceptible, is noticed and rejoiced over. Zephaniah 3:17 says, *The Lord thy God in the midst of thee is mighty; he will save, he will rejoice over thee with joy; he will rest in his love, he will joy over thee with singing.*

We stagger under such a thought and cry, "Oh, but Lord, how can You possibly find beauty in *me*? How can You ever rejoice in *me*? I am so small, so stunted, so far from mature."

Tenderly He draws near and whispers into our hearts, "Child, it's because you are mine. It's because I am at work in you. I know the potential."

✳   ✳   ✳

Despite God's tender whispers, I still get agitated sometimes about my spiritual growth. If only I could speed up the process, pass over the laws of time, and immediately become all God wants me to be! But you know what? It's not going to happen. My agitation actually hinders growth.

Okay, so I shouldn't be agitated. Does that mean I can sit back and be content to never grow? Absolutely not! If growth is absent from my life, death is sure to follow. I can't stay stagnant.

If agitation is out, and so is apathy, then what *am* I supposed to do? God's Word speaks into my dilemma: *Being confident of this very thing, that he which hath begun a good work in you will perform it until the day of Jesus Christ* (Philippians 1:6).

Ah! there's the answer: trust God for the process. Gone will be my agitation, as I rest in the fact that my God is trustworthy, His time-frame perfect, His ability unhindered, His work sure. Gone will be my apathy, for confidence stirs up a vibrant, compelling zeal in me.

He who first drew me to Christ will draw me onward. He who is Alpha and Omega will never begin a work only to let it die. However slow the growth process may seem, I can find rest and beauty on the way. There will be a completion—for me *and* for you.

What About You?

Because we are still weak humans, our way through life can seem long and ugly at times. Why not pour out your fears, struggles, and concerns to God right now? Ask Him to take over. Shift the weight of responsibility onto His capable shoulders. Then take the time to seek out and write down several points of beauty God is revealing to you in *your* growth process (maybe it's the deeper understanding of an attribute of God, the fresh discovery of an eternal promise, or the joyous blessing of an answered prayer). Now go out with zeal, eager to bring glory to God by growing in Him!

_____

_____

_____

_____

_____

Seeking Knowledge

Let's put our whole hearts into learning more about the spiritual growth process God is bringing us through. And let's be encouraged.

Find the Meaning: Look up the word *process* and write out the definition.

_____

_____

_____

Let the Light In: Read Philippians 3:12-14.
- What is an honest assessment of my Christian life?

_____

_____

_____

_____

- What should my response be nevertheless?

_____

_____

_____

_____

Now read Psalm 138:8, Psalm 37:5b, and I Corinthians 1:8.

- What is God's part in my growth process?

_____

_____

_____

_____

- What is mine (read Psalm 37:5a and also Colossians 1:29)?

_____

_____

_____

_____

Last of all, read II Corinthians 4:16 and Philippians 3:20-21.

- How is it possible for me to discover fresh beauty and purpose along the way (II Corinthians 4:16)?

_____

_____

_____

_____

- When the growth process is finally over, what will my full completion be (Philippians 3:20-21)?

_____

_____

_____

_____

Adopt a Motto: The process of growth is a process of beauty.

Ponder a Prayer:
"…Renew our courage for the way;
New life, new strength, new happiness,
We ask of Thee; oh, hear, and bless!"

Johann Rist

Afterword

So here we are at the end of our fruit of the Spirit study. I can testify I've learned so much! God is opening my heart to a deeper understanding (and experience!) of the abundant life He has made possible for me. I hope you are experiencing the same thing.

But please, let's not stop here. I want to encourage you to keep on studying, to keep on learning, to keep on yielding, and to keep on growing. God has so much more for us!

And now, as I bring this book to a close, my prayer for you is that, *The grace of the Lord Jesus Christ, and the love of God, and the communion of the Holy Ghost, be with you all. Amen* (II Corinthians 13:14).